d
g
Lace

Anja van Laar

FORTE PUBLISHERS

© 2005 Forte Uitgevers, Utrecht
© 2005 for the translation by the publisher
Original title:
Achtergrondembossing met kant

All rights reserved.
No part of this publication may be copied, stored in an electronic file or made public, in any form or in any way whatsoever, either electronically, mechanically, by photocopying or any other form of recording, without the publisher's prior written permission.

ISBN 90 5877 633 6

This is a publication from
Forte Publishers BV
P.O. Box 1394
3500 BJ Utrecht
The Netherlands

For more information about the creative books available from Forte Publishers: www.forteuitgevers.nl

Final editing: Gina Kors-Lambers, Steenwijk, the Netherlands
Photography and digital image editing: Fotografie Gerhard Witteveen, Apeldoorn, the Netherlands
Cover and inner design: BADE creatieve communicatie, Baarn, the Netherlands
Translation: Michael Ford, TextCase, Hilversum, the Netherlands

Contents

Preface	3
Techniques	4
Step-by-step	5
Materials	6
Aubergine	7
Romantic cards	10
Blue	13
Say it with... stripes	16
1-2-3D	18
A baby	21
Anemones	24
Christmas	27
Patterns	31

Preface

Hello everybody,

Have you also not had enough of embossing yet? I certainly haven't. I have designed another two stencils, which are excellent to use with the other background embossing stencils. In this book, I have only used the latest four stencils with frames, but if you find your old stencils, you will see that they also go very nicely with the new stencils.

Once you have embossed the new stencils and cut out the pattern, the result looks just like lace. This is the reason why this book is called *Background Embossing with Lace*. I hope you will have lot of fun embossing.

Good luck!
Anja

Many thanks to everybody at home who, once again, has been very patient and given me lots of help.

Techniques

Embossing
Place the stencil on the good side of the card. Turn the stencil and the card over, place them on a light box and use the embossing stylus to copy the illuminated shapes. If you wish, use Pergasoft (Pergamano) to make the embossing easier. If you are going to emboss a large area, then lightly rub a candle over the card.

To prevent lines and scratches when embossing vellum, carefully start with a circular movement and then increase the pressure until the vellum goes white. For a larger pattern, start with a large embossing stylus in the middle and then go along the edges with a smaller stylus.

Embossing and cutting using the lace stencils
Emboss the edge and then turn the card and stencil over. Use a propelling pencil to mark the lines and the middle pieces which are to be cut out. Place the ruler along the straight lines and cut them. Next, position the card so that you can cut all the curves which point in the same direction without having to keep moving the card. Turn the card a quarter of a revolution and cut the other curves. Use a knife to prick out the middle pieces. If necessary, carefully rub out any pencil lines which remain.

3D cutting
Cut the entire picture out for the first layer. For the next layer, decide what is in the background and do not cut that out. Cut out as many layers as you want in this way. If you do not use many layers, cut the incisions far into the paper and cut the front parts out completely. You can add as much or as little glue as you wish under the pictures, depending on the depth that you wish to create. If you put the glue in a syringe, you will have more control over the quantity you apply.

Step-by-step

1. Emboss the lace and draw the outline of the parts to be cut out.

2. Use a ruler to cut the straight lines.

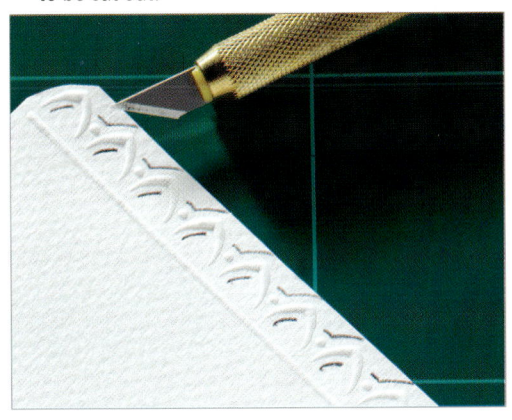

3. Cut the curves.

4. Rotate the card slightly. Cut the other curves and use a knife to remove the small pieces.

Materials

- Card: Papicolor, Mi-Teintes and cArt-us
- Making Memories card and vellum
- Pergamano vellum and parchment
- K&Company Stripe flat paper
- Cutting sheets: Dimensions, Mattie, 1-2-3D, Picturel, Picturel Step by Step and Marjoleine
- Embossing stencils: AE 1214 to AE 1219
- Circle cutter
- Hole punch
- Light box
- Embossing stylus
- Knife
- Cutting mat
- Power Pritt
- Silicon glue
- 3D scissors
- Shaping pen
- Shaping mat
- Xyron 150
- Label Art
- Coluzzle mini label template
- Eyelet hammer
- Eyelet tool
- Eyelet mat
- Eyelets
- Ribbon and cord
- Funny Ribbons

Aubergine

What you need
- Card: Papicolor - snow white 30, Metallic - aubergine 146 (thin) and Perkacolor - candy pink 150 (thin)
- Cutting sheets: Dimensions DM 0104 and 0105
- Embossing stencils: AE 1216 and 1219
- Organza ribbon
- Double sided adhesive tape

What you need

1. Make an aubergine double card (18 x 12.5 cm). Take a piece of white card (18 x 10.5 cm) and use stencil 1219 to emboss the lace on two sides. Cut out the middle pieces, cut along the edges and stick it on the card.

2. Take a piece of candy pink card (18 x 7 cm). Use stencil no. 1216 to emboss the background and stick the sticker on it. Use a glue pen to stick it on a piece of white card (18 x 7 cm).

3. Take a piece of Organza ribbon. Fold it around the card and use double-sided adhesive tape to stick it to the back. Stick this on the card and make the pictures 3D.

Good luck

What you need
- Card: Papicolor - snow white 30, Metallic - aubergine 146 (thin) and Perkacolor - candy pink 150 (thin)
- Cutting sheets: Dimensions DM 0104 and 0105
- Embossing stencils: AE 1217 and 1218
- Eyelets: gold
- Label Art
- Pearl cord: gold (small)

Instructions
1. Take a piece of white card (21.5 x 17 cm) and fold it 9 cm from the left-hand side. Use stencil no. 1218 to emboss the lace. Cut out the middle pieces and cut along the edge. Take a piece of candy pink card (17 x 6.5 cm). Use stencil no. 1217 to emboss the background and use a glue pen to stick it on the card.

2. Take a piece of aubergine card (24.5 x 17 cm). Fold it 12 cm from the right-hand side and stick the larger half to the back of the white card. Add some decorative stickers and the picture. Use the pearl cord to attach the label to the tulip.

3. Use Label Art to make a label from aubergine and candy pink card and punch a gold eyelet in it. Use gold cord to attach the label to the card. Use a small piece of adhesive tape to stick the ends of the cord to the back of the card.

Large bow

What you need
- Card: Papicolor - snow white 30, Metallic - aubergine 146 (thin) and Perkacolor - candy pink 150 (thin)
- Cutting sheets: Dimensions DM 0104 and 0105
- Embossing stencils: AE 1215 and 1218
- Eyelets: gold
- Pearl cord: pink
- Organza ribbon

Instructions
1. Take a piece of white card (25.5 x 13.5 cm) and fold it 12 cm from the left-hand side. Use stencil no. 1218 to emboss the lace twice and cut out the middle pieces. Take a piece of candy pink card (13.5 x 10 cm) and fold it 1 cm from the left-hand side. Use stencil no. 1215 to emboss the background and stick the card to the back of the card.

2. Take a piece of Metallic aubergine card (13.5 x 13.5 cm) and stick it inside the card next to the fold applying glue to only a small strip of the card.

3. Use aubergine and candy pink card to make a label and punch a gold eyelet in it.

4. Stick the picture on the card. Use gold cord to attach the label to the card. Use a hole punch to punch two holes in the fold of the card and thread a bow made of Organza ribbon and a piece of pink pearl cord through them.

Romantic cards

Good luck

What you need
- Mi-Teintes card: ivory 111
- Making Memories card: large rose brick and stripes
- Making Memories vellum: berry
- Embossing stencils: AE 1217 and 1218
- Eyelets: gold
- Coluzzle template: mini labels
- Rub-ons: metallic
- Waxed cord: natural (1 mm)

Instructions

1. Take a piece of Making Memories card (21.5 x 13.5 cm) and fold it 8 cm from the left-hand side. Take a piece of ivory card (13.5 x 9.5 cm) and use stencil 1218 to emboss the lace. Cut out the middle pieces, cut along the edge and stick it behind the front of the card.

2. Take a piece of berry vellum (13.5 x 13.5 cm) and use stencil 1217 to emboss dots on it. Use Power Pritt to stick it behind the front of the card.

3. Use the mini label template to make two labels out of striped and ivory card. Emboss the lace on the ivory label and cut the middle pieces out.

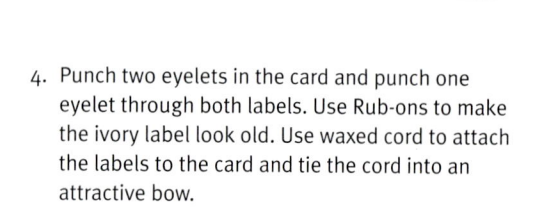

4. Punch two eyelets in the card and punch one eyelet through both labels. Use Rub-ons to make the ivory label look old. Use waxed cord to attach the labels to the card and tie the cord into an attractive bow.

Congratulations

Instructions

1. Take a piece of floral card (22 x 13.5 cm) and fold it 8.5 cm from the left-hand side. Take a piece of striped card (13.5 x 13.5 cm) and stick it behind the front of the card next to the fold on the left-hand side applying glue to only a small strip of the card.

2. Take a piece of ivory card (13.5 x 10 cm) and use stencil 1219 to emboss the lace. Cut out the middle pieces and cut along the edge. Stick it behind the front of the card. Take a piece of self-adhesive ribbon (13.5 cm) and stick it on the card.

3. Use striped and ivory card to make two labels. Use Rub-ons to decorate the ivory label.

4. Punch one eyelet through both labels and punch two eyelets in the card. Use green, waxed cord to attach the labels to the card and tie the cord into an attractive bow.

What you need
- Mi-Teintes card: ivory 111
- Making Memories card: small rose and stripes
- Embossing stencil: AE 1219
- Eyelets: gold
- Coluzzle template: mini labels
- Rub-ons: metallic
- Waxed cord: green (1 mm)
- Funny Ribbons

Large ribbon

Instructions

1. Take a piece of ivory card (20 x 13.5 cm) and fold it 6.5 cm from the left-hand side. Use stencil no. 1218 to emboss the lace. Cut out the middle pieces and cut along the edge.

2. Take a piece of berry vellum (13.5 x 6.5 cm) and fold it 1.5 cm from the left-hand side. Use stencil no. 1216 to emboss the background. Use Power Pritt to stick the vellum to the rear of the card.

3. Take a piece of floral card (13.5 x 13.5 cm) and stick it behind the front of the card.

4. Use a hole punch to punch two holes in the fold. Thread Organza ribbon through the holes, tie the ribbon into an attractive bow and also thread two pieces of pearl cord through it.

What you need
- Mi-Teintes card: ivory 111
- Making Memories card: large rose brick
- Making Memories vellum: berry
- Embossing stencils: AE 1216 and 1218
- Organza ribbon: ivory (2 cm)
- Pearl cord: white

Blue

Get well soon

What you need
- Card: Papicolor - snow white 30 and night blue 41, Antica - denim 165 (thin) and Perkaline - amber 153
- Embossing stencil: AE 1218
- Mattie cutting sheets
- Decorative stickers

Instructions

1. Make a night blue double card (17 x 10.5 cm) with the fold at the top and stick a piece of denim card (17 x 5.3 cm) on it 1.5 cm from the bottom.

2. Take a piece of snow white card (17 x 5.3 cm) and use stencil 1218 to emboss the lace twice. Cut out the middle pieces, cut along the edges and stick it on the card.

3. Take a piece of amber card (17 x 2.2 cm) and stick it on the card.

4. Stick decorative stickers and the picture on the card. Make the picture 3D.

Kingfisher

Instructions
1. Make a night blue double card (13 x 13 cm) with the fold on the left-and side and stick a piece of denim card (13 x 12.5 cm) on it.

2. Take a piece of snow white card (13 x 12 cm). Use stencil no. 1218 to emboss the lace on the right-hand edge and stencil no. 1214 to emboss the background on the 6.5 cm wide strip of card on the left-hand side and stick it on the card. Take a piece of amber card (13 x 4 cm) and stick it on the card.

3. Use Label Art to make a night blue, a denim and an amber label. Use one eyelet to attach all the labels together and punch two eyelets in the card. Use Organza ribbon to attach the labels to the card and tie the ribbon into an attractive bow.

4. Stick pictures on the card and on the label and make them 3D.

What you need
- Card: Papicolor - snow white 30 and night blue 41, Antica - denim 165 (thin) and Perkaline - amber 153
- Embossing stencils: AE 1214 and 1218
- Mattie cutting sheets
- Eyelets: gold
- Organza ribbon: navy blue (6 mm)
- Label Art

Collage card

Instructions

1. Make a night blue double card (13 x 13 cm) with the fold at the top and stick a piece of denim card (13 x 7.2 cm) on it 3 mm from the bottom. Take a piece of snow white card (13 x 7.2 cm) and use stencil 1219 to emboss the lace twice. Cut out the middle pieces, cut along the edges and stick it on the card. Take a piece of amber card (13 x 4.3 cm) and stick it on top.

2. Take a piece of denim card (7 x 5 cm), a piece of snow white card (6.5 x 4.5 cm) and a piece of amber card (6 x 4 cm) and stick them on top of each other in the top right-hand corner of the card 3 mm from the edge.

3. Take a piece of snow white card (5 x 5 cm) and use stencil no. 1216 to emboss the background on it. Stick it in the top left-hand corner of the card 3 mm from the edges and punch two silver eyelets in it. Thread Organza ribbon through the eyelets, tie the ribbon into an attractive bow and attach a silver Charm to it.

4. Stick the pictures on the card and make them 3D.

What you need
- Card: Papicolor - snow white 30 and night blue 41, Antica - denim 165 (thin) and Perkaline - amber 153
- Embossing stencils: AE 1216 and 1219
- Mattie cutting sheets
- Eyelets: silver
- Organza ribbon: navy blue (6 mm)
- Charm: silver

Say it with... stripes

Rose

What you need
- Mi-Teintes card: white 335
- Making Memories vellum: berry
- K&Company Stripe flat paper
- Embossing stencil: AE 1219
- Picturel Step by Step cutting sheet
- Circle cutter

Instructions

1. Make a white double card (13.5 x 13.5 cm) and stick a piece of striped card (13 x 13 cm) on it.

2. Take a piece of white card (10 x 10 cm) and use stencil 1219 to emboss the lace on two sides. Cut out the middle pieces, cut along the edges and stick it on berry vellum (10 x 10 cm). Stick this at an angle on the card.

3. Cut a circle (Ø 6.5 cm) from striped card. Stick the picture (from which the middle has been cut out) on it and stick it on the card.

4. Make the picture 3D.

Gift envelope

Instructions
1. Use white card to make a white envelope according to pattern 1. Stick striped card (16.2 x 9 cm) on the long straight side.

2. Take a piece of white card (15 x 7 cm) and use stencil 1218 to emboss the lace on two sides. Cut out the middle pieces, cut along the edges and stick it on berry vellum (15 x 7.5 cm). Stick this at an angle on the gift envelope.

3. Stick a picture on top and make it 3D.

What you need
- *Mi-Teintes card: white 335*
- *Making Memories vellum: berry*
- *K&Company Stripe flat paper*
- *Embossing stencil: AE 1218*
- *Picturel Step by Step cutting sheet*
- *Pattern 1 (page 31)*

1-2-3D

Congratulations

What you need
- Mi-Teintes card: red earth 130, salmon 384 and white 335
- Embossing stencil: AE 1219
- Cutting sheet: 1-2-3D
- Stickles: Icicle

Instructions
1. Make a red earth double card (13.5 x 13.5 cm) and stick a piece of white card (13.5 x 11 cm) on it.

2. Take a piece of salmon card (13.5 x 10.5 cm) and use stencil 1219 to emboss the lace twice. Cut out the middle pieces, cut along the edges and stick it on the card.

3. Stick the picture on the card and make it 3D. Add some glitter.

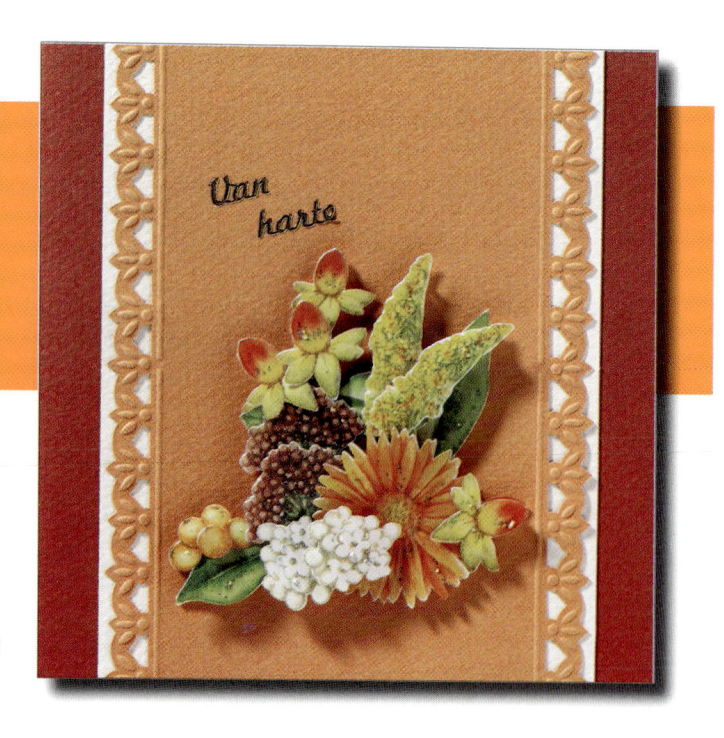

Bouquet

Instructions
1. Take a piece of salmon card (25.5 x 13.5 cm) and fold it 12 cm from the left-hand side. Use stencil no. 1218 to emboss the lace and stencil 1215 to emboss the background. Cut out the middle pieces and cut along the edge.

2. Take a piece of red earth card (13.5 x 13.5 cm) and stick it inside the card on the right-hand side next to the fold applying glue to only a small strip of the card.

3. Take a piece of white card (13.5 x 12 cm) and stick it inside the card on the left-hand side next to the fold applying glue to only a small strip of the card.

4. Stick the picture on the card and make it 3D. Add some glitter.

What you need
- *Mi-Teintes card: red earth 130, salmon 384 and white 335*
- *Embossing stencils: AE 1215 and 1218*
- *Cutting sheet: 1-2-3D*
- *Stickles: Icicle*

Wreath

What you need
- Mi-Teintes card: red earth 130, salmon 384 and white 335
- Embossing stencil: AE 1218
- Cutting sheet: 1-2-3D
- Stickles: Icicle

Instructions

1. Make a red earth double card (13.5 x 13.5 cm) with the fold on the left-hand side.

2. Take a piece of white card (13.5 x 11 cm) and use stencil 1218 to emboss the lace on two sides. Cut out the middle pieces, cut along the edges and stick it on the card 5 mm from the left-hand side.

3. Take a piece of salmon card (13.5 x 8.3 cm) and stick it on the card.

4. Stick the picture on the card and make it 3D. Add some glitter.

A baby

Bottle

What you need
- Card: Papicolor - snow white 30, Perla - golden yellow 141 (thin), Perkacolor - mist152 (thin) and Antica - blue rain 171 (thin)
- Embossing stencils: AE 1214 and 1219
- Cutting sheets: 1-2-3D
- Organza ribbon: white (3 mm)
- Charms
- Patterns 2, 3 and 4 (pages 31 and 32)

Instructions
1. Make a white card according to pattern 3. Take a piece of golden yellow card (13.5 x 7.5 cm). Use stencil no. 1214 to emboss the background on it and stick it on the card.

2. Use stencil no. 1219 to emboss the lace on the right-hand side. Cut out the middle pieces and cut along the edge. Take a piece of blue rain card (12 x 6.2 cm) and stick it on the card.

3. Use mist card to make the envelope according to pattern 2 and use a small amount of Power Pritt to stick it on the card.

4. Use golden yellow card to make the bottle according to pattern 4. Use Organza ribbon to tie an attractive bow around the bottle and attach a Charm to it.

A baby

Instructions

1. Take a piece of golden yellow card (23.5 x 13 cm) and make two zigzag folds 6.5 cm and 11.5 cm from the left-hand side. Use stencil no. 1218 to emboss the lace and stencil 1214 to emboss the background on the right-hand side. Cut out the middle pieces and cut along the edge.

2. Take a piece of blue rain card (13 x 12 cm) and stick it behind the right-hand side.

3. Use mist card to make the envelope according to pattern 2. Use chalks to colour the edges and use a small amount of Power Pritt to stick it on the card.

4. Use stencil 1214 to emboss the heart on white card and cut it out leaving a border. Stick it on blue rain card and cut it out leaving a border. Use the hole punch to punch a hole in the heart and thread Organza ribbon through it.

What you need
- Card: Papicolor - snow white 30, Perla - golden yellow 141 (thin), Perkacolor - mist 152 (thin) and Antica - blue rain 171 (thin)
- Embossing stencils: AE 1214 and 1218
- Cutting sheets: 1-2-3D
- Organza ribbon: white (3 mm)
- Chalks
- Pattern 2 (page 31)

Booties

Instructions

1. Take a piece of white card (29.6 x 10.5 cm) and make zigzag folds 7.3 cm and 10.8 cm from the left and right-hand sides. Use stencil no. 1219 to emboss the lace on the left and right-hand sides. Cut out the middle pieces and cut along the edges. Take two pieces of golden yellow card (10.5 x 5.5 cm). Use stencil no. 1217 to emboss the background on it and stick it on the card.

2. Cut a blue rain circle (Ø 10.5 cm) and a golden yellow circle (Ø 10 cm). Stick them together and then stick them in the middle of the card. Use Label Art to make a mist label and a blue rain label. Use stencil no. 1218 to emboss the lace on the mist label. Cut out the middle pieces and cut along the edge.

3. Punch one eyelet through both labels and punch two eyelets in the card. Use Organza ribbon to tie an attractive bow and use it to attach the labels to the card.

4. Stick the pictures on the card and make them 3D.

What you need
- Card: Papicolor - snow white 30, Perla - golden yellow 141 (thin), Perkacolor - mist 152 (thin) and Antica - blue rain 171 (thin)
- Embossing stencils: AE 1217 and 1219
- Cutting sheets: 1-2-3D
- Circle cutter
- Label Art
- Eyelets: gold
- Organza ribbon: white (3 mm)

Anemones

Label card

What you need
- Mi-Teintes card: white 335
- cArt-us card: warm pink 485
- Pergamano vellum: striped
- Embossing stencils: AE 1216 and 1219
- Marjoleine cutting sheet
- Waxed cord: green
- Eyelets: gold

Instructions

1. Make a white double card (13.5 x 13.5 cm) and use stencil 1219 to emboss the lace on the right-hand side 1.5 cm from the edge. Cut out the middle pieces and cut along the edge. Stick the picture on the card and cut out the middle pieces of the picture. Use stencil no. 1216 to emboss the background

2. Take a piece of striped vellum (13.5 x 13.5 cm) and stick it inside the card on the left-hand side next to the fold applying glue to only a small strip of the card.

3. Use stencil no. 1216 to emboss the label on the white card and cut it out leaving a border. Stick it on warm pink card and cut it out leaving a border. Punch an eyelet in the label and two eyelets in the card.

4. Use waxed cord to attach the label to the card and tie the cord into an attractive bow.

Quadriptych

Instructions

1. Take a piece of warm pink card (28.8 x 7.2 cm). Make zigzag folds 7.2 cm, 14.4 cm and 21.6 cm from the left-hand side. Use stencil 1215 to emboss the square twice on white card. Cut out the middle pieces and cut along the edge. Stick the squares on the first and third flaps from the left. Stick the pictures on almond green card (4.4 x 4.4 cm) and then stick them on the squares.

2. Take two pieces of parchment (6.5 x 4.5 cm) and tear the top half off at an angle. Use stencil no. 1215 to emboss dots on the parchment. Use chalks to colour the torn edges. Use three eyelets to attach each piece to the card.

3. Take two pieces of white card (5.5 x 4.5 cm). Use stencil no. 1218 to emboss the lace on the right-hand side of one piece and on the left-hand side of the other piece. Cut out the middle pieces and cut along the edge. Stick them on almond green card (5.5 x 4.5 cm). Punch an eyelet in the labels and thread a piece of waxed cord through them.

What you need
- Mi-Teintes card: white 335 and almond green 480
- cArt-us card: warm pink 485
- Pergamano parchment: 150 grams
- Embossing stencils: AE 1215 and 1218
- Marjoleine cutting sheet
- Waxed cord: green
- Chalks
- Eyelets: gold

Folding card

Instructions
1. Make a white double card (13.5 x 13.5 cm). Use stencil no. 1215 to emboss a square in the middle of the left-hand inside of the card and cut out the middle pieces.

2. Use a scoring pen to make two folding lines in the middle of the front of the card. Cut around the right-hand side of the square and fold the front flap over. Use stencil no. 1218 to emboss the lace. Cut out the middle pieces and cut along the edge. Use stencil no. 1215 to emboss the background.

3. Cut warm pink card to the correct size and stick it behind the front flap which has been folded over (also behind the square).

4. Take a piece of striped vellum (13.5 x 13.5 cm) and stick it inside the card on the right-hand side next to the fold applying glue to only a small strip of the card. Stick the picture on almond green card (4.4 x 4.4 cm) and stick it on the card.

What you need
- Mi-Teintes card: white 335 and almond green 480
- cArt-us card: warm pink 485
- Pergamano vellum: striped
- Embossing stencils: AE 1215 and 1218
- Marjoleine cutting sheet

Christmas

Bells

What you need
- Mi-Teintes card: red earth 130, white 335, dark green 448 and apple green 475
- Making Memories vellum: willow
- Embossing stencils: AE 1215 and 1218
- Picturel Step by Step cutting sheets
- Organza ribbon: green (2 cm)

Instructions
1. Make an apple green double card (14.8 x 14.8 cm).

2. Take a piece of willow vellum (14.8 x 7.5 cm). Use stencil no. 1215 to emboss dots on it, except for a 1.5 cm wide strip on the left-hand side. Stick the vellum on the card by only applying glue to the 1.5 cm wide strip.

3. Take a piece of white card (14.8 x 7.5 cm) and use stencil 1218 to emboss the lace. Cut out the middle pieces and cut along the edge. Stick it on red earth card (14.8 x 7.8 cm) and then on dark green card (14.8 x 8.3 cm).

4. Fold Organza ribbon around it. Use double-sided adhesive tape to stick it on the card.

Merry Christmas

What you need
- *Mi-Teintes card: red earth 130, white 335 and apple green 475*
- *Making Memories vellum: willow*
- *Embossing stencils: AE 1215 and 1218*
- *Picturel Step by Step cutting sheets*
- *Organza ribbon: white (3 mm)*
- *Eyelets: gold*
- *Coluzzle template: mini labels*
- *Funny Ribbons*
- *Xyron 150*

Instructions

1. Make an apple green double card (14.8 x 14.8 cm). Take a piece of willow vellum (14.5 x 14.5 cm) and use stencil 1215 to emboss the background. Use Power Pritt to stick the vellum on the card.

2. Cut a triangle from red earth card. Cut a white strip (29.6 x 5.5 cm). Place the strip on the triangle and cut it to size. Use stencil no. 1218 to emboss and cut the lace. Cut along the edge and stick it on the triangle. Stick a piece of Funny Ribbons on the card. Use stencil no. 1218 to emboss stripes on the triangle and stick it on the card.

3. Use the mini label template to make labels from willow vellum, white card and red earth card. Use the Xyron sticker maker to apply an adhesive layer to the vellum label and stick it on the white label. Punch eyelets in the labels and the card.

4. Use Organza ribbon to attach the labels to the card and tie the ribbon into an attractive ribbon. Stick a picture on the card and make it 3D.

Bow

What you need
- Mi-Teintes card: red earth 130, white 335, dark green 448 and apple green 475
- Making Memories vellum: willow
- Embossing stencils: AE 1216, 1217 and 1219
- Picturel Step by Step cutting sheets
- Organza ribbon: green (2 cm)
- Pearl cord: white

Instructions

1. Make an apple green double card (14.8 x 14.8 cm). Take a piece of willow vellum (7.9 x 6.2 cm) and use stencil no. 1216 to emboss the background on it. Use Power Pritt to stick it in the bottom left-hand corner 3 mm from the sides.

2. Take a piece of red earth card (7.9 x 7.7 cm) and stick it in the bottom right-hand corner 3 mm from the sides. Take a piece of white card (7.9 x 7.7 cm) and use stencil 1219 to emboss the lace. Cut out the middle pieces, cut along the edge and stick it on the card.

3. Take a piece of red earth card (5.5 x 4.5 cm) and use stencil no. 1217 to emboss the background on it. Stick it on dark green card (6 x 5 cm) and then stick it in the top right-hand corner 3 mm from the sides. Take a piece of white card (8.9 x 6 cm) and use stencil no. 1216 to emboss the background on it.

4. Fold a piece of Organza ribbon around the card. Make a double knot at the front and tie two pieces of pearl cord in it. Stick everything in the top left-hand corner of the card 3 mm from the sides.

Card on page 1

What you need
- Mi-Teintes card: ivory 111
- Making Memories card: large rose brick and stripes
- Making Memories vellum: berry
- Embossing stencil: AE 1219

Instructions

1. Make a striped double card (13.5 x 13.5 cm) and stick berry vellum (13.5 x 8 cm) on it by only applying glue in the middle.

2. Take a piece of ivory card (13.5 x 7.5 cm) and use stencil 1219 to emboss the lace. Cut out the middle pieces, cut along the edge and stick it on the card.

3. Take a strip of floral card (13.5 x 4.3 cm) and stick it on the card.

4. Cut out a rose. Use silicon glue to stick it on the card and make it 3D.

Card on page 3

What you need
- Mi-Teintes card: white 335
- Making Memories vellum: berry
- K&Company Stripe flat paper
- Embossing stencils: AE 1217 and 1218
- Picturel Step by Step cutting sheet
- Eyelets: gold
- Waxed cord: natural (1 mm)
- Coluzzle template: mini labels
- Xyron 150

Instructions

1. Make a white double card (13.5 x 13.5 cm). Use stencil no. 1218 to emboss the lace diagonally through the middle. Cut out the middle pieces and cut along the edge. Stick striped card (13.5 x 13.5 cm) behind the front flap.

2. Cut a triangle from berry vellum (bottom and left-hand sides are 13.2 cm). Use stencil no. 1217 to emboss some dots on it and use Power Pritt to stick it on the card.

3. Use the mini label template to make a label from white card and a label from berry vellum. Use the Xyron sticker label to apply an adhesive layer to the vellum label and stick it on the white label. Punch two eyelets in the card and one eyelet in the label. Use waxed cord to attach the label to the card and tie the cord into an attractive bow.

4. Stick the picture on the card and make it 3D.

Pattern 1: Gift envelope
Increase in size by 200%

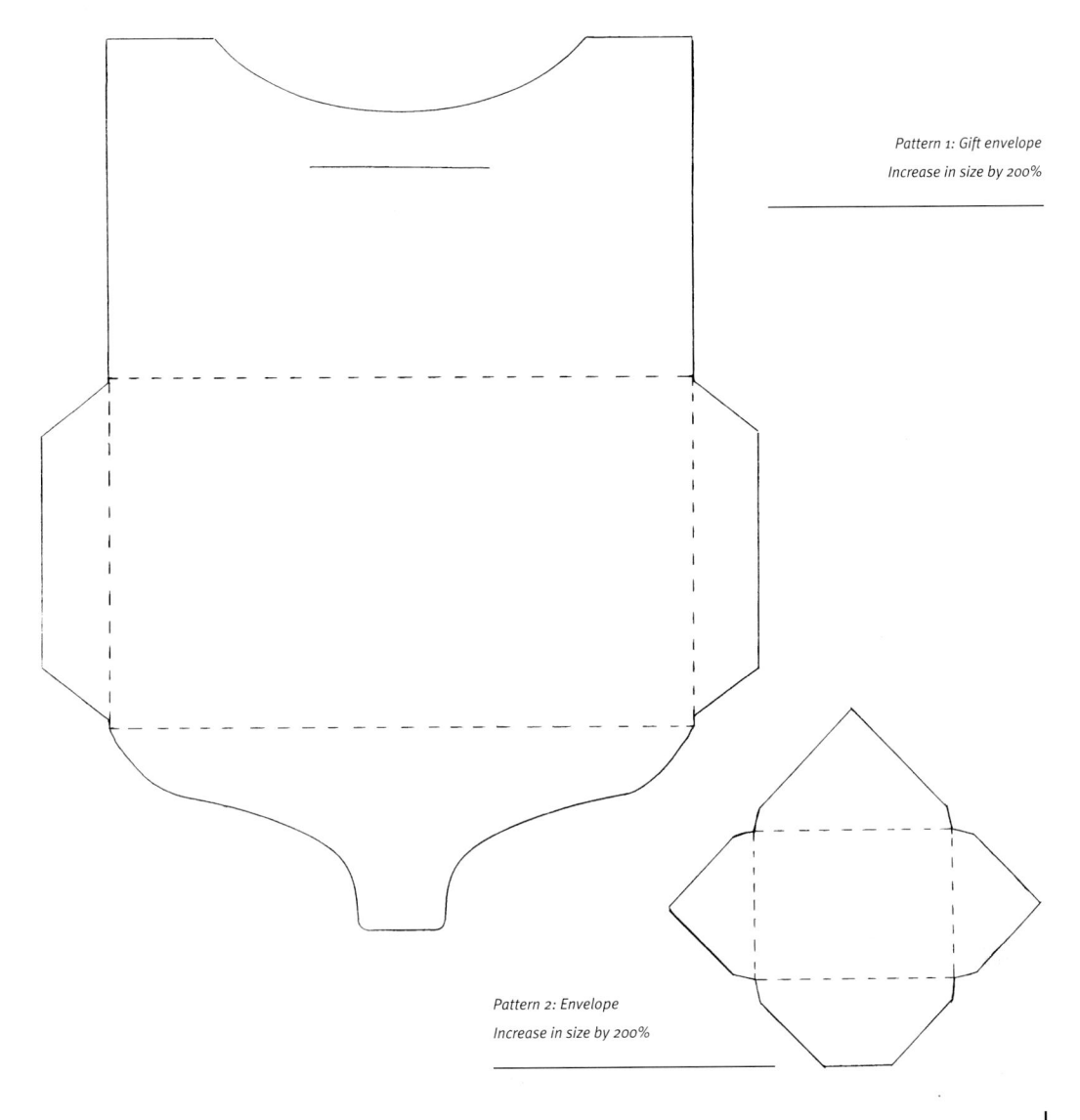

Pattern 2: Envelope
Increase in size by 200%

Pattern 3: Increase in size by 200%

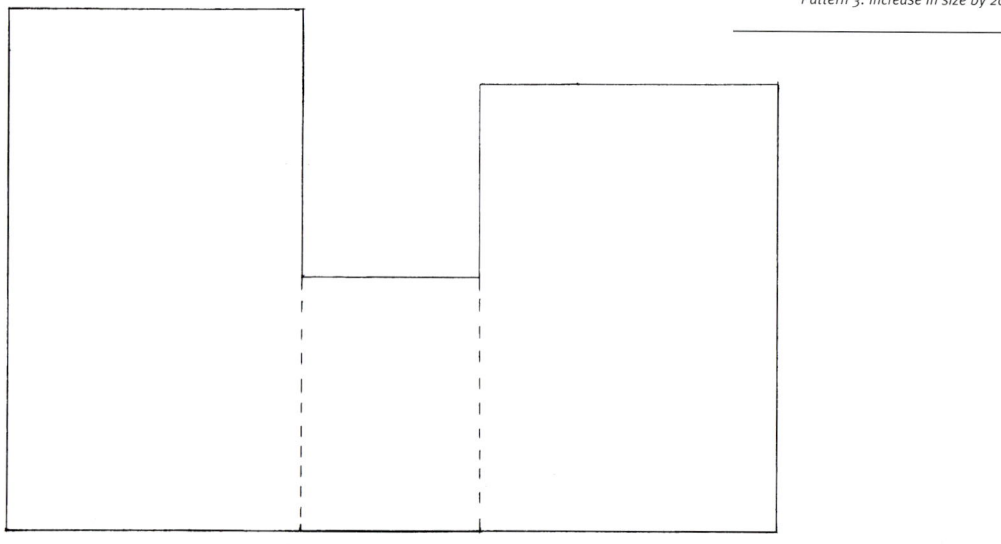

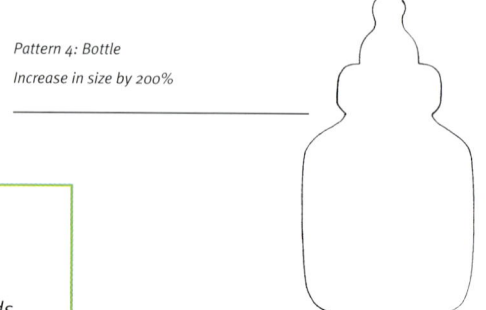

Pattern 4: Bottle
Increase in size by 200%

Many thanks for providing the material:
Avec B.V. in Waalwijk, the Netherlands
Kars & Co BV in Ochten, the Netherlands.
Papicolor International B.V. in Utrecht, the Netherlands.